drive by

car rides through the night sky
a backdrop of stars
blinking street lights steering
the tilted flash of a mirror
reclining into the headrest
after a day of empty seatbelts
highways hairpin turns
radio dialed up to a whisper

welcome mat

conversations happen
through a one-sided window
all esteem necessary
scattered room with dated picture frames
magnets on the fridge proclaim:
happy holiday cards
shadows cast
from tasteful streamers tucked
into cluttered drawers
crumpled receipts
from months made invisible

night walks
ice-encrusted branches
forming frames in the
sky. muffling gnarled
trees
dragging through snow
in a shadowy rake
silent, glittering
footfalls
sound wrapped in
wisps of condensation
circuit strings
of bursting icicle light
bulbs
full of crackling static

crunching copper wire
warped glass shade of
lowered blinds
turning headlights
pave over glittering
potholes
decades of driveways
still need fixing

cement mixtures never
match
paint swatches
long since sold out
breath chilled by each
bootprint
sharp flakes fall into
irritation,
freezing over just as
fast
every flicker of a
silhouette
places a curse on each
ornament

by the fireplace
gas burner blue flames blink
a whistle of snow
wrapped around the chimney
tired sweater sleeves huddling closer
over a steaming ceramic mug
should've used a coaster
impressions of condensed water
imprinted on hard floors

liminal
scorching lenses in rectangular light
dry, cracking among support beams
bouncing conversations won't echo back
waterfall of crunching styrofoam
those peaceful droplets can crush skulls

limbs full of sand
sifting through laundry
shifting glances linger
on each part of the room
leathery wings outstretched
a flash as gone as it began
cross-referencing matching numbers
listed descriptions of drawings
it all means something in a cypher of myth

refrigerator
drumming clink of glasses
bottles set side by side. lined up
an army, a wall
fortress behind painted rooms &
fine china cabinets
dusted glasses & display plates
magnets & postcards decorated with
accidental sharpie designs
dents from swinging doors too far

glasses more than half emptied
crumpled over tile crying
photos in an album that was never taken

alarm clock
clawing out of the imprint in my mattress
there's a crack in the watch face
every creak & groan of a footstep
alternating stretches of sun & moon
jumpy with each raised voice–
any threat of breaking glass
weights sewn like nightmare stars into linen
seconds clicking in place with each toss
turning grass golden again

volume check
dials slide from left to right
half-arc swing of sound
undercut by raging bass
floorboards blanket wrapped in earphones
accidental flick of a finger
misplaced sentences crack speakers

tv
couches offer comfort
especially when you're not used to warmth
clad in slippers wandering downstairs
propped up by a fortress of potato chips
cans or residual soda glasses
hugged in wrap around sound

candle in a cold room
whispers of shadows shuddering
moonbeams highlight the doorframe
creeping curtains climbing
crackle of a light switch
click of fluorescent bulbs
flickering lightning bugs sleep
guarded by cupped hands
clenched like a prayer
letting dreams drift out
quietly
to join the stars

bike

spires of light from spinning tires
clicking chain a hissing air tube
reflectors tossing bright dots & street grit
specks of glass melted down
glittering with each step up to the curb

having another episode
an open cabinet
a studied reflection
my face looks vague
features are familiar enough
lean close enough to hear the walls
lines of navy border tiles
past the occasional scuttling
speck of shadow scrambling
back into the other side of the glass
tracked by smudges on the mirror
looking for anything uneven to wake up

don't look at me
heads swivel so fast at the flash of a phone
something peers through
the small glass circle
retreat among a world that's been replaced
thoughts can't bridge a disconnected body
sense of dread with a hollowed out alarm

shadow foundry
melting down my nightmares
deep velvet with empty matter
gritty as it's poured out
feeding the creatures crouched in corners
shapes or forms in and out of eyesight
underlining dark circles
eyeshadows don't lose a certain look
going without radio silence
shifting with internal temperatures

there's a quiet at the end of a high
stapled telephone poles
of torn corner messages
hangnail remnants of rain-soaked fliers
droplets of seeping ink circles
propping up by a numbing shoulder
shifting pockets & skittish glances
solitude of four walls
where clouds can obscure faces
no one but rerunning white noise

gore
i took out my intestines
to wind them around my arms
embroidered sleeves
heartstring sinew
adorn the collar of my blood-stained shirt
staunched with packing layers of dirt

bloodletting

stuck to the floor
for the first time without humidity
mosquitoes hum a few feet from starving
feedback of reflections & instant pictures
bears no resemblance
to the months that slip past
could be anyone in the passing years
place markers provide vague reminders
camera rolls
more reliable than the mind
sometimes
someone today fades into tomorrow
hairline cracks torn &
reassembled through tape
scorching noise feeds fire
dried out trees until they crack
uprooted in a misplaced patch of sparks
storm of red
getaway trails gone in days

need some sunglasses
measured in forkfuls of ultraviolet
steady adjustments over bridges
forecasted waves spinning surroundings
torn fan blades of silver slices. whispered
mechanical whirring
day punctuated with melodic shudders &
thudding of heavy machinery

i'm the only ghost in this store

fluorescents refuse to fade patterns
clothing stuck in bold
vibrant colors these lights won't wash out
while carts continue to turn corners
people nestled in conversations.
are we looking over my shoulder or yours?
tracking lists when writing reads jumbled
these boxes seem too bright
it's too bright & the logos can't read back

couldn't really call it decorating

one year i etched an indent into my bedroom floor
it was all started by the reverberations of dropping things
like the half-moon scratches of my fingernails
something so satisfying about a motion down in solid lines
easy to hide under a plush carpet
blends well with the seams of wooden floorboards

home
pin up at each place setting
everything on a stage, homemade
comfortably draped in olive paint
neutral & earthy easy to wash down
digestible. sugar-coated finishes
always watch what they all might think
looking over now
steps along a tripwire. always
present behind sentences. pretenses
shield of normalcy unblemished
dependency on the finest compliments
compliant & clean

storage
model train sets
paper mountains of mache tracks
nearly glued dust mites
spray painted grass
pull cord ladder plastic sealed
with containers
over-flooded with styrofoam flakes of snow
clothing decorated with wrinkled linen

spares
snapped frames caught in tangled teeth
wires in a wicker basket
craft store cloth lining
loose change collected near an air vent
weathered pennies
pieces of metal flavored dust mites
tucked into shards of scattered plates

falling leaves
the sun beams. bleeding
midway into the sky
cooling soil
dug deep orange of a setting moon
withering on tangles of stems
season when fruits peel
a bite into bitter ends

time to unwind
cleaning blankets wave
like flags in the sunlight
dust mites dislodged from carpeted floor
cross-legged empty eyes against a tv screen
clamor of dishes being sizzled. setting tables
corrected crooked picture frames
kept away from polished silverware drawers

writing down the date
numbers were only made
for headings on paper
pages form the words for days & months
tracking in ledgers.
since slipped through fingers
bound spirals into calendars
back when all clocks stopped
before daylight was invented

wanting to peel my skin off
drawing dotted lines with a pen
scissors don't cut right angles
catching instead
no smooth glide through wrapping paper
folded at all the uncomfortable angles
disorienting scotch tape sides
mismatched & glittering
creased, folded in twists
doubled up ribbons
paper jammed until closed off circulation

bent light rays
reaching through the mirror
a twisting arm tucked behind my head
invisible haze
an ill-defined panel
pushback from this portal
folded paper sheet
faded pencil lines
keeping back a shaky scream

nine to five
intentions sandwiched between filing cabinets
manila panels dividing a new demeanor
telephone tone lines stay busy
radios heavy with static that never breaks, only blurs

gravestones

stacks of worn cardboard
push across the floor & dark ink
scribbled through with markers
heavy from mildew
rotting beams reach up into the attic
strain of a ceiling
dirt drumming
like fingers against coffin lids
cotton-insulated conversations &
footsteps six feet under a resounding bell

ferris wheel

embroidered but still boring
with neon lights in slow spirals
nowhere close to spinning
painfully still to my knotted stomach
preferred roller coasters to life dragging
i can't hear the chain crank
From under the car
up here unsettled
without white knuckles against gravity

water boiled by drowning
movements stuck fast. a stick in wet sand
soaked to the toenails
blankets of rain rise sour
cloudburst of a colorful oil spill
rattles bubble up. creeping through metal
pipe
in a propped open door frame
air conditioner garrote
cut off with the start of a fan

humming fans
airflow like a tangle of blankets
folding over each imbalance
chattering radio announcements
tension held up by shoulder blades
thumbtacks of glossy posters
bright colors with phrases
cheering on the daylights
wedged like stones lodged in the sole of a shoe

Made in the USA
Columbia, SC
29 April 2022